Acorn Woodpeckers

Studies For Wildlife Artists

Photography and Text

by

Al Lodwick

Printed in The United States of America.

First Edition 2015

ISBN 978-1512139303

Dedication

To Ann Lodwick, my wife and best friend for the past thirty-seven years.

Acknowledgements

Scott Mies for encouragement and editorial advice.

Rachel Lodwick for the Mieswick, LLC logo.

Victoria Tubbs for the author's photograph.

Introduction

This book is the result of five years of nature photography in the biologically diverse central highlands of Arizona around Prescott These are not what most people first imagine when they think of Arizona. At its lowest levels you find desert grassland. This gives way to Oak-Pinon-Juniper woodland. Higher still are the tall Ponderosa Pines – a stand of trees stretching for hundreds of miles in Arizona and New Mexico. At the highest levels you find Douglas Fir forest. Here you find an intermingling of flora and fauna from both hotter and colder environments. For example, you can find hedgehog cacti growing near the roots of Ponderosa Pines.

In this environment lives the aptly-named Acorn Woodpecker. It gathers acorns from the Oaks and stores them in holes drilled primarily into Ponderosa Pines. However, they will also store acorns in other trees that also have "soft" wood such as Alligator Junipers.

The emphasis of this book is to depict scenes for wildlife artists that are not easily captured with the un-aided eye. Examples of this are what Acorn Woodpeckers do when they take flight from a vertical tree trunk and the acrobatics they perform when chasing insects. Just as these are not easily seen, they are difficult to photograph. Sometimes, the photographs are out-of-focus but are included anyhow for the depiction of, for example, the shape of wings and tail in flight.

Photographs of the environment surrounding the homes of the Acorn Woodpeckers are included for artists wishing to include these details in their work. The text also describes the habits of Acorn Woodpeckers.

The author hopes that non-artists will also enjoy the pictures and learn more about Acorn Woodpeckers and the central highlands of Arizona.

Al Lodwick
Prescott, Arizona
May 2015

FEMALES

Female Acorn Woodpeckers are easily distinguished from males by their smaller red cap that touches a black band on their forehead. The red cap of the male touches white on the forehead. Acorn Woodpeckers live in family groups of up to twenty birds. Usually they will only be seen singly or in pairs.

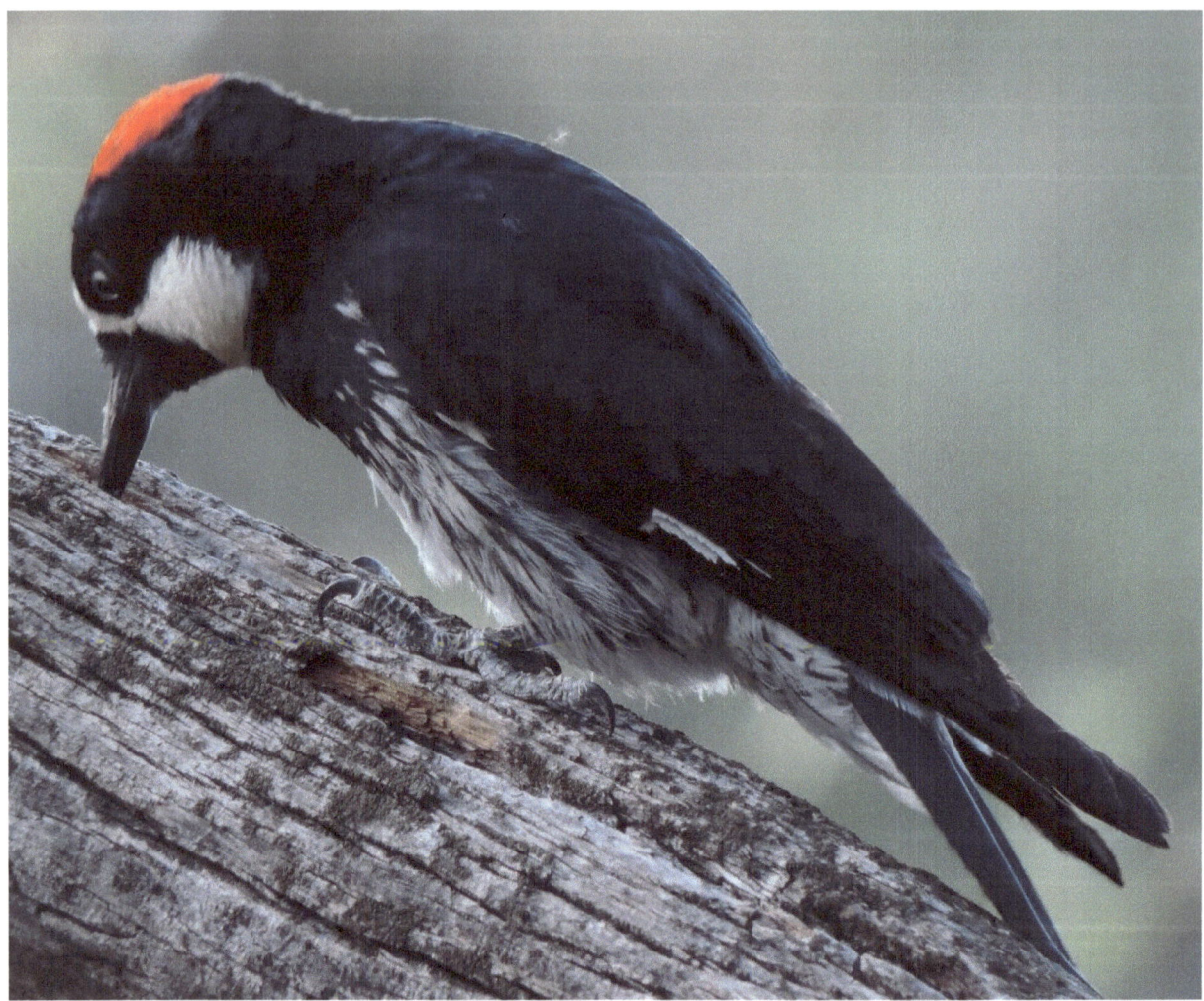

A female Acorn Woodpecker is seeking insects in a dead Ponderosa Pine tree that has partially collapsed onto a neighboring tree. Note the large feet and claws. Here you can also see the angle at which the legs extend from the body. Also note the tail feathers touching the tree. These feathers are very stiff and function somewhat as a third leg providing additional stability when a hole is being pecked out.

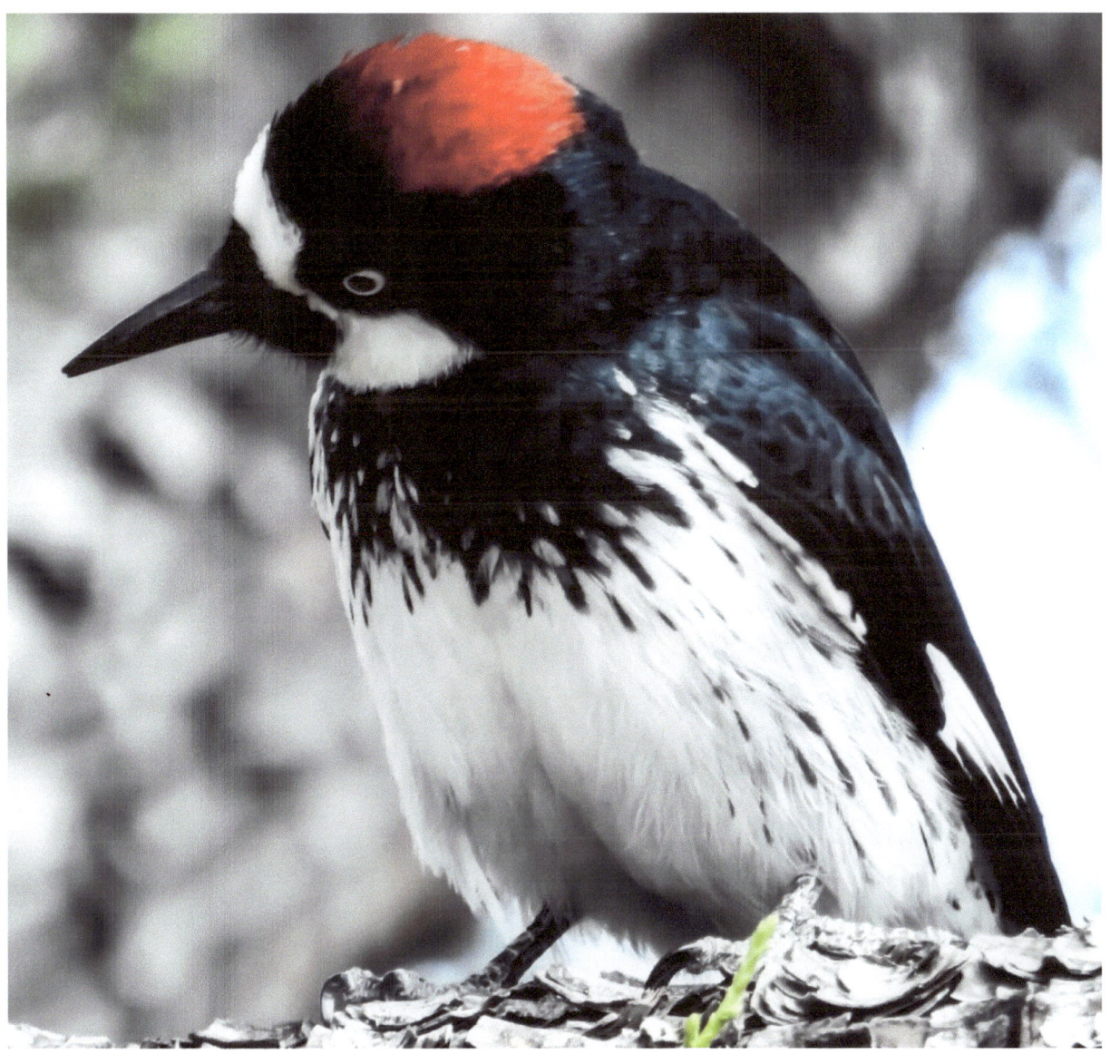

This picture shows a female Acorn Woodpecker sitting on a horizontal limb of an Alligator Juniper tree. The tree gets its name from the bark resembling the hide of an alligator. You can see the coloring of the breast and the white wing bar.

The overall length of an adult Acorn Woodpecker is a little over 8 inches. For comparison, this is the length of the short side of one page of this book. It weighs about 3 ounces. That is about the weight of the cooked meat in a quarter-pound burger.

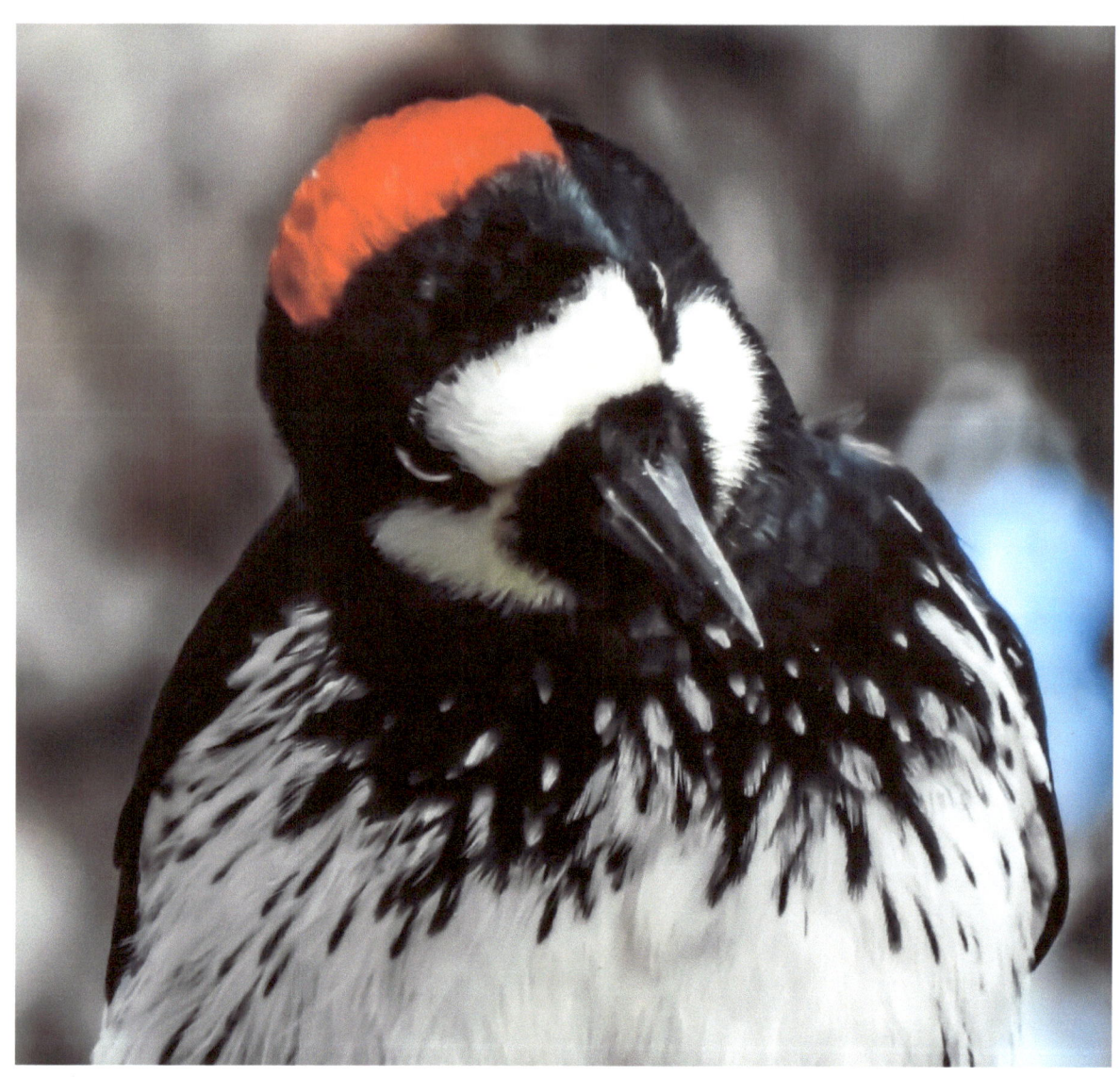

Note the extremely sharp point of the chisel-like beak.

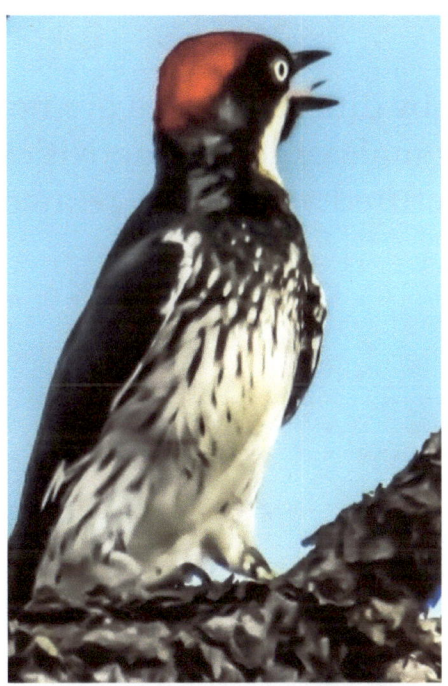

This female illustrates how the tongue protrudes when it is calling.

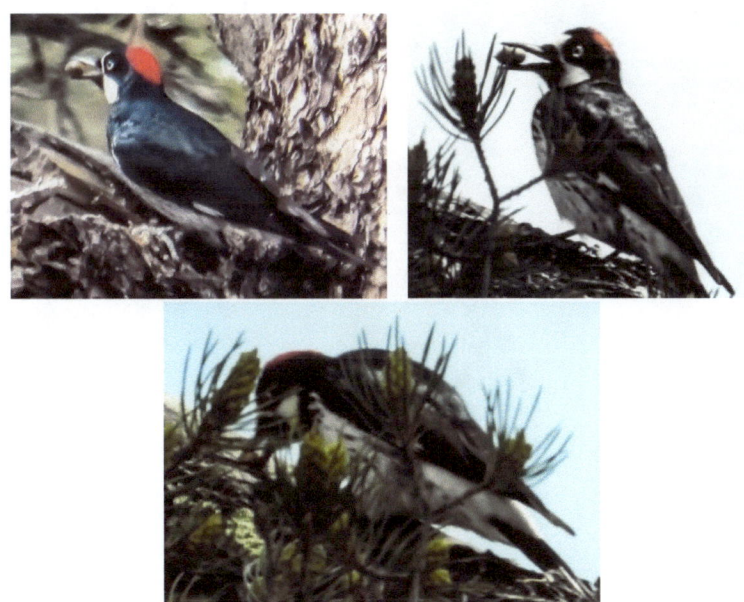

Even though these pictures are not sharply focused, they illustrate the size of an acorn that an Acorn Woodpecker is able to carry and place into a previously excavated cavity. For more detail on acorns see the "Environment" section of this book.

MALES

The actions depicted by different sexes are not meant to imply that these are specifically male or female activities. The author thinks that the activities pictured were more related to chance than any other factor.

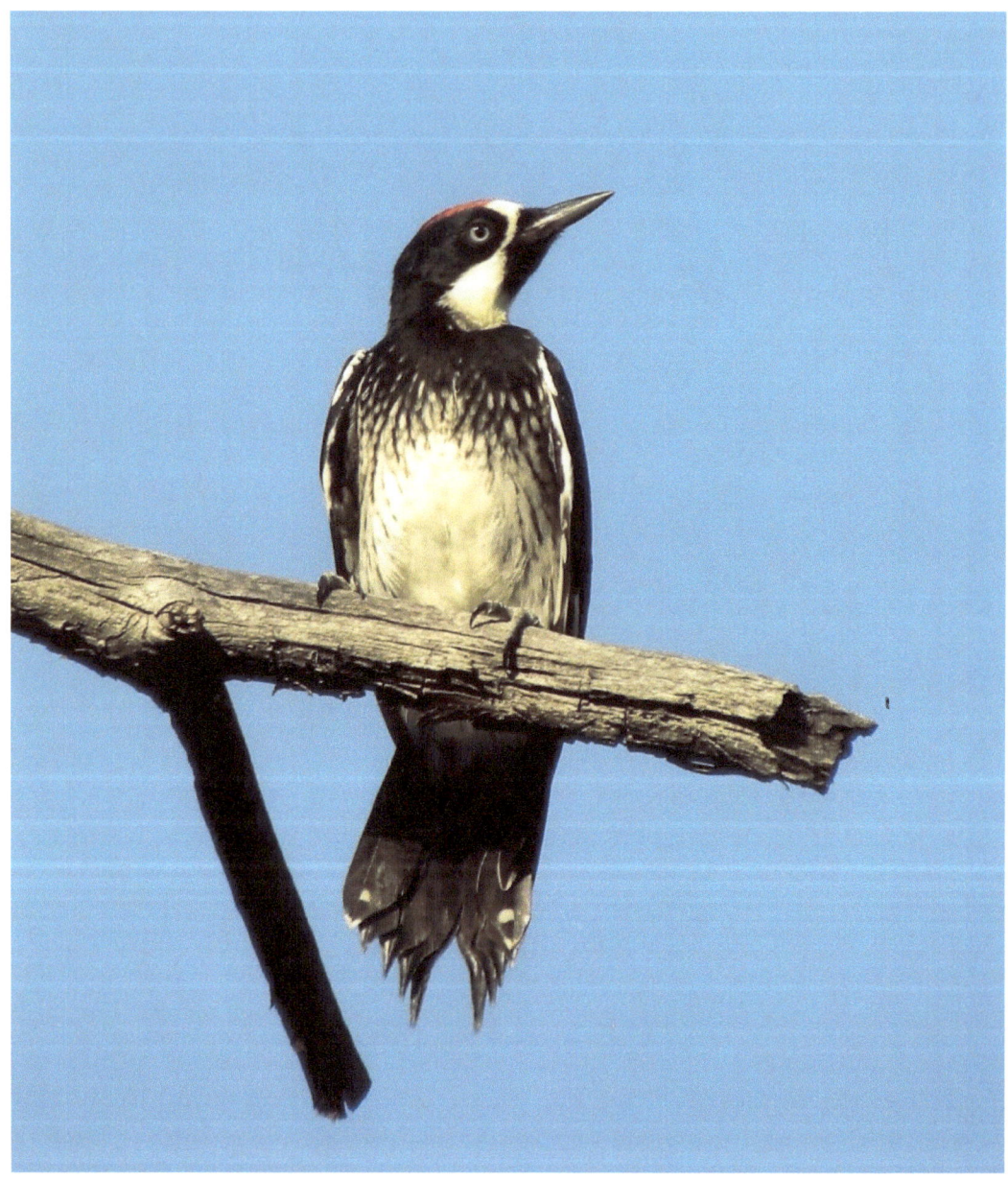

In this picture note the five stiff feathers on each side of the tail and the placement of the feet on a small horizontal tree limb.

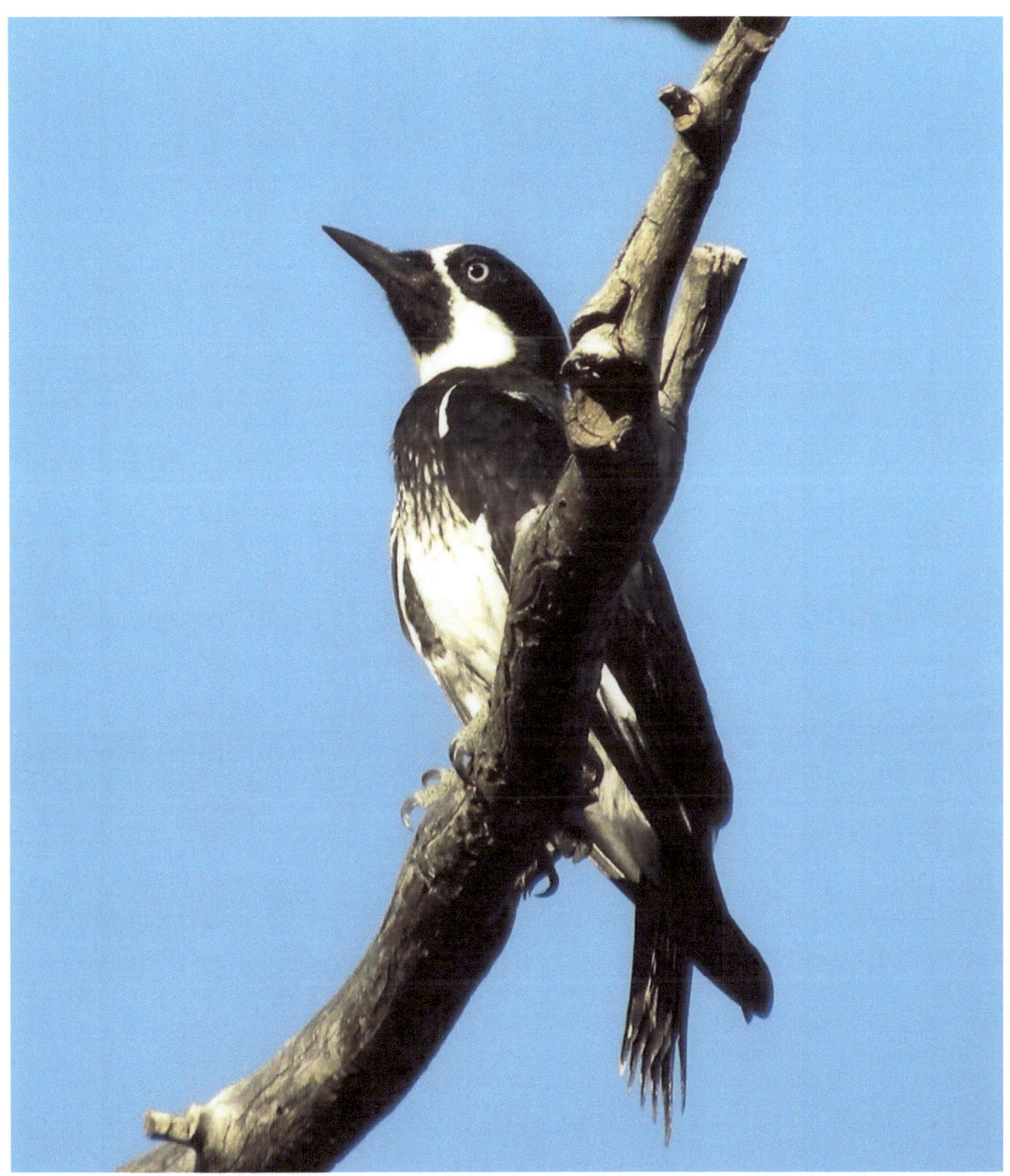

In addition to noting the position of the feet and tail, take a close look at the underside of the limb on which the Acorn Woodpecker is sitting. The design that seems to be carved into the wood near the bird's feet are trails created by the Ips Bark Beetle. This beetle took advantage of the weakened Ponderosa Pines during the drought of 2002 to multiply rapidly and prey on the trees. A fungus carried by the beetles probably was the agent directly responsible for the tree's death. You may show a similar pattern when depicting dead trees.

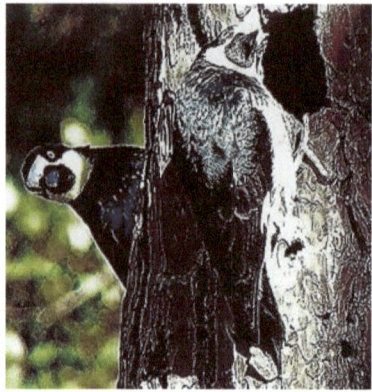

These two male acorn woodpeckers appear startled by what one of them has just discovered in a nesting hole in a dead Ponderosa Pine.

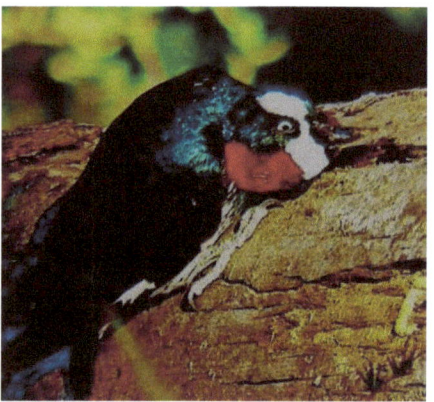

Many birds are able to rotate their head about 180 degrees. This one was picking ants out of a fallen Ponderosa Pine log. When he could not find any more, he decided to look in the crack. Evidently his eyes are developed to see what is overhead better than what is below him. In order to see better he rotated his head. A few seconds later he flew away.

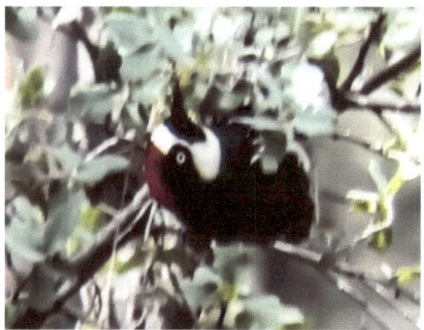

When harvesting acorns, an Acorn Woodpecker is may hang upside down.

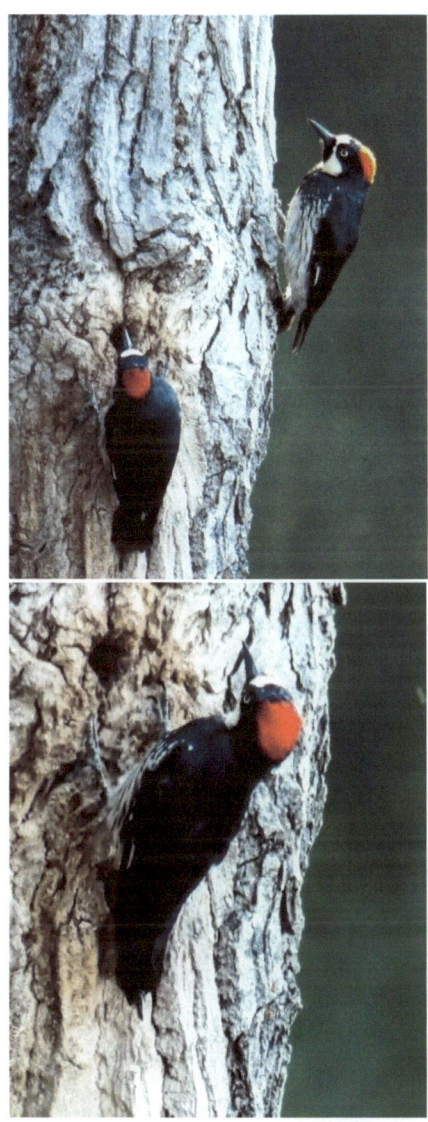

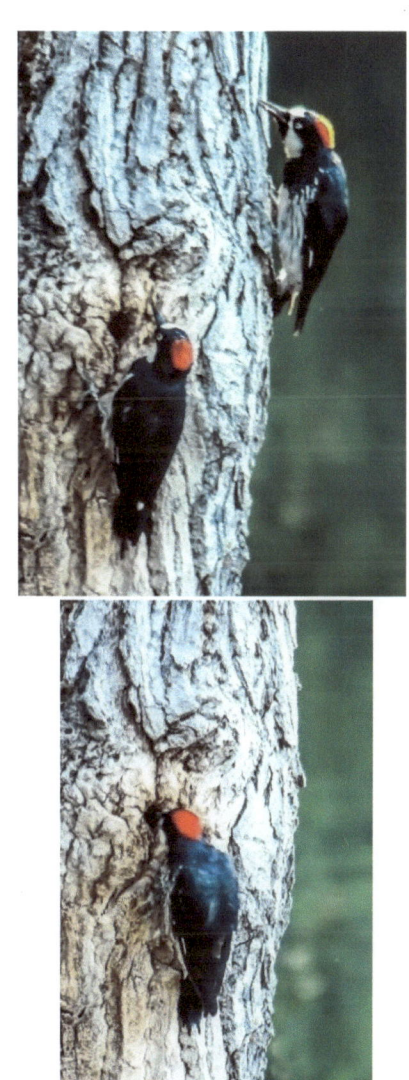

Besides acorns, the birds also eat insects. This is especially true in spring and early summer when the supply of acorns runs low. Tree sap is found in the cambium layer which is just under the bark of trees. They appear to have chiseled through the bark to get at the sugar-laden sap of an Arizona White Oak. There may also be some insects in the hole, caught in the sticky sap. Oak wood is very hard so they do not usually make a hole big enough for nesting in oak trees.

FLIGHT

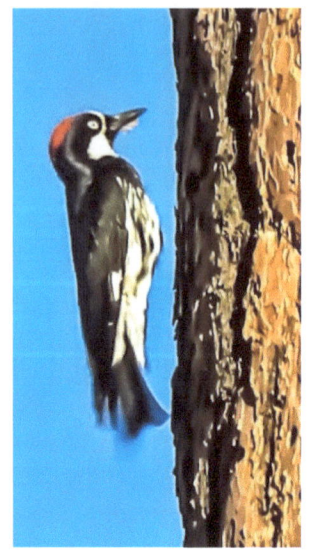

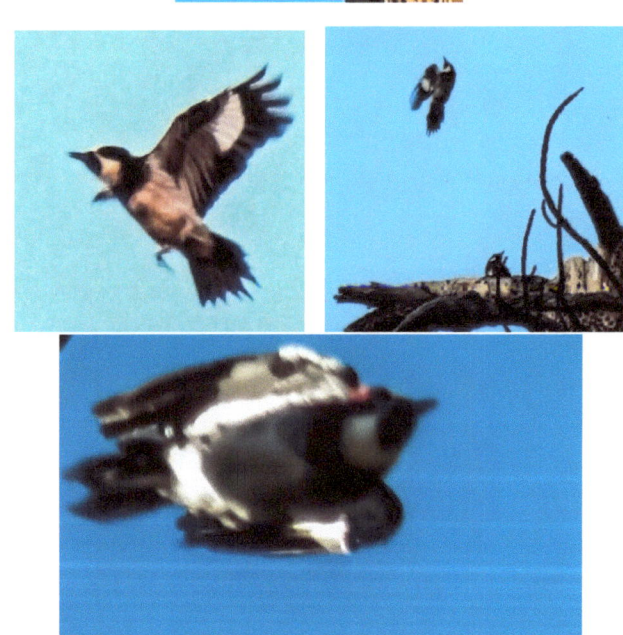

Acorn Woodpeckers are powerful fliers. In the top picture note that the bird is not attached to the tree. When taking-off from a vertical surface she simply jumps backward and flaps her wings.

When Acorn Woodpeckers are doing "acrobatic" flying they broaden their tails as seen in the middle two pictures. When they are in their "speed" mode, the tail feathers are held much closer together. In either mode there is a noticeable "V" to the tail.

In flight they show a white wing patch on both wings and a white rump patch.

ENVIRONMENT

PONDEROSA PINES

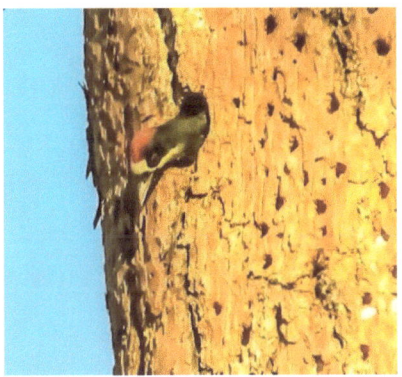

This male Acorn Woodpecker is emerging from a nesting cavity. The young are born in the spring when there are few acorns available for food. Consequently, they are fed mainly insects. Both males and females, will participate in raising the young.

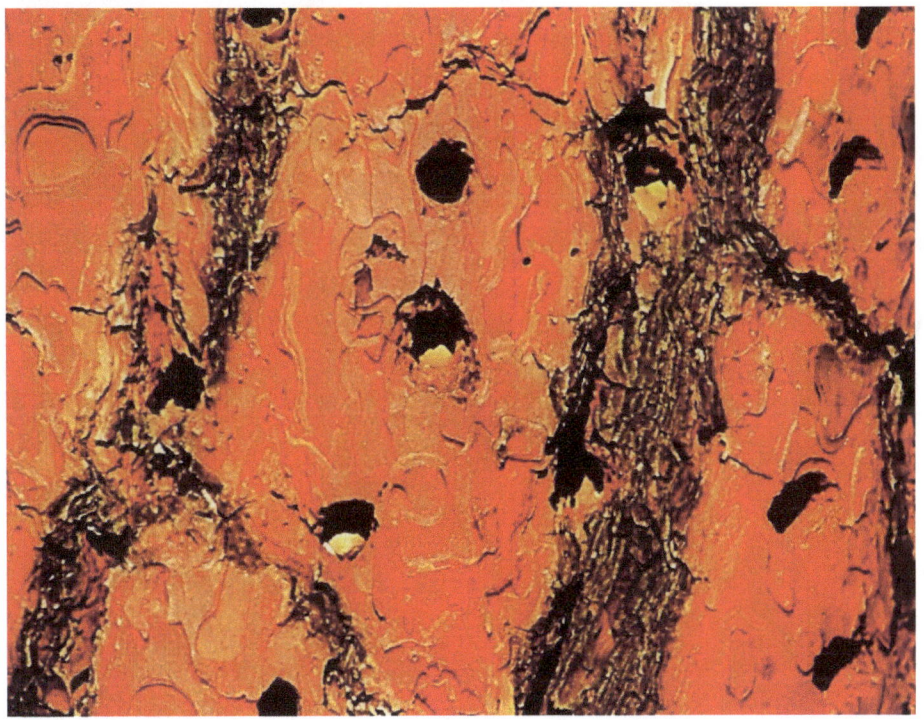

Acorn Woodpeckers have been reported to store as many as 50,000 acorns in one Ponderosa Pine. These are referred to as granary trees. Some internet sources seem to imply that they only do this in California but the author has observed many such trees in Arizona. Note the acorns in the holes.

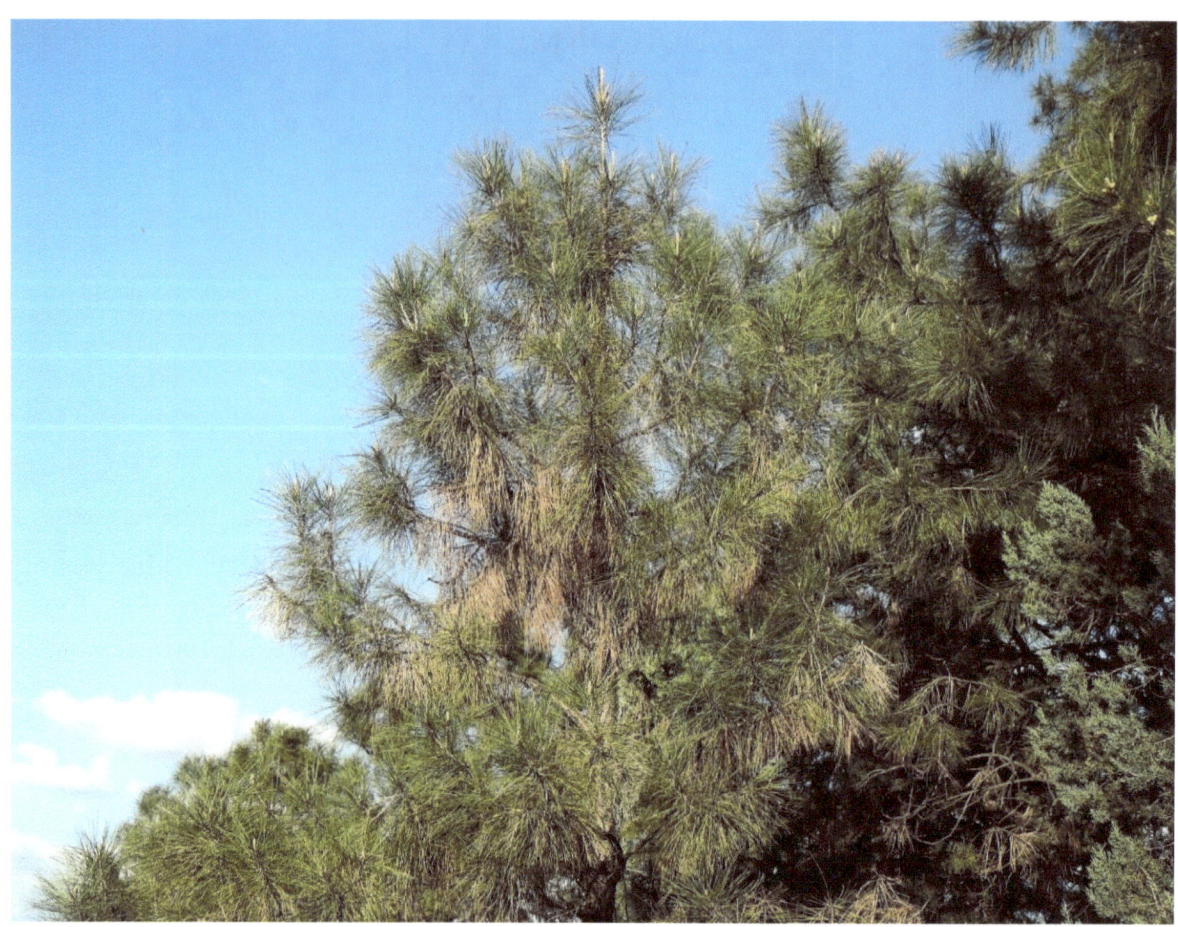

This shows the growth candles and normal needle die-off of a Ponderosa Pine tree. The needles are leaves. Unlike deciduous trees that lose all of their leaves every year, healthy Ponderosa Pine will lose about 30% of its needles each year. On average, the needles that fall to the ground will take a little more than two years to completely decay. You will see a lot of needles on the ground in a Ponderosa woodland.

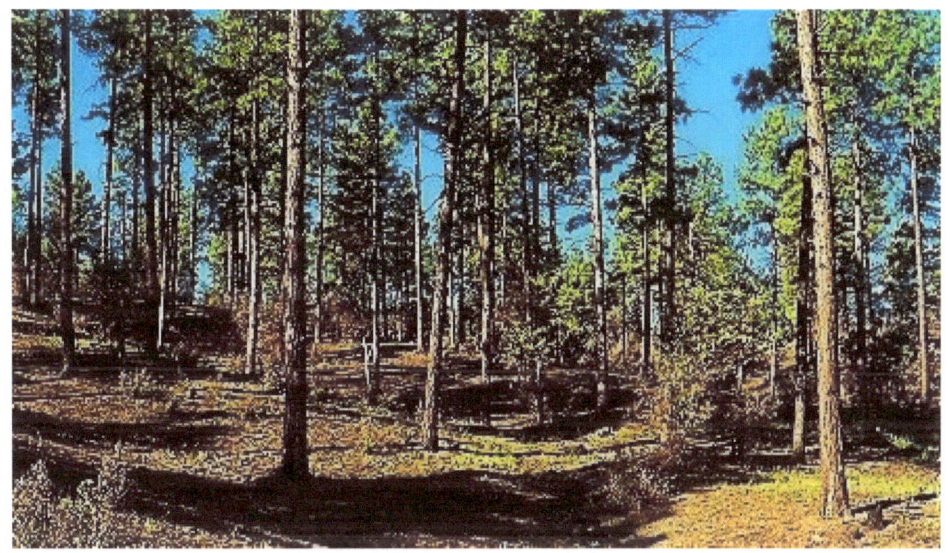

The early pioneers recorded that a horse and wagon could easily be driven through a Ponderosa Pine woodland. A woodland has trees that grow nearly straight up allowing for the sky to be visible. A forest has trees that spread their branches to form a canopy resulting in only occasional views of the sky. These trees could easily stand 50 feet tall. On a healthy tree with adequate space the outline of the green branches should appear as a triangle starting about 20% of the way up the trunk.

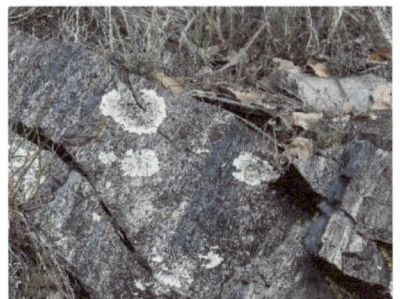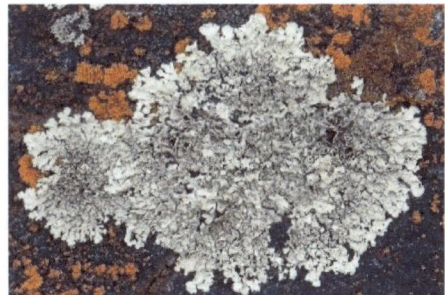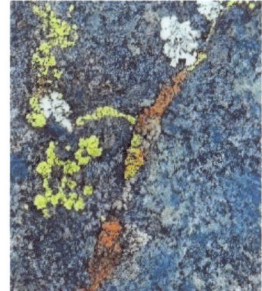

If you choose to depict a Ponderosa Pine woodland, you can add some interesting detail by adding rocks that have patches of lichens like these covering them.

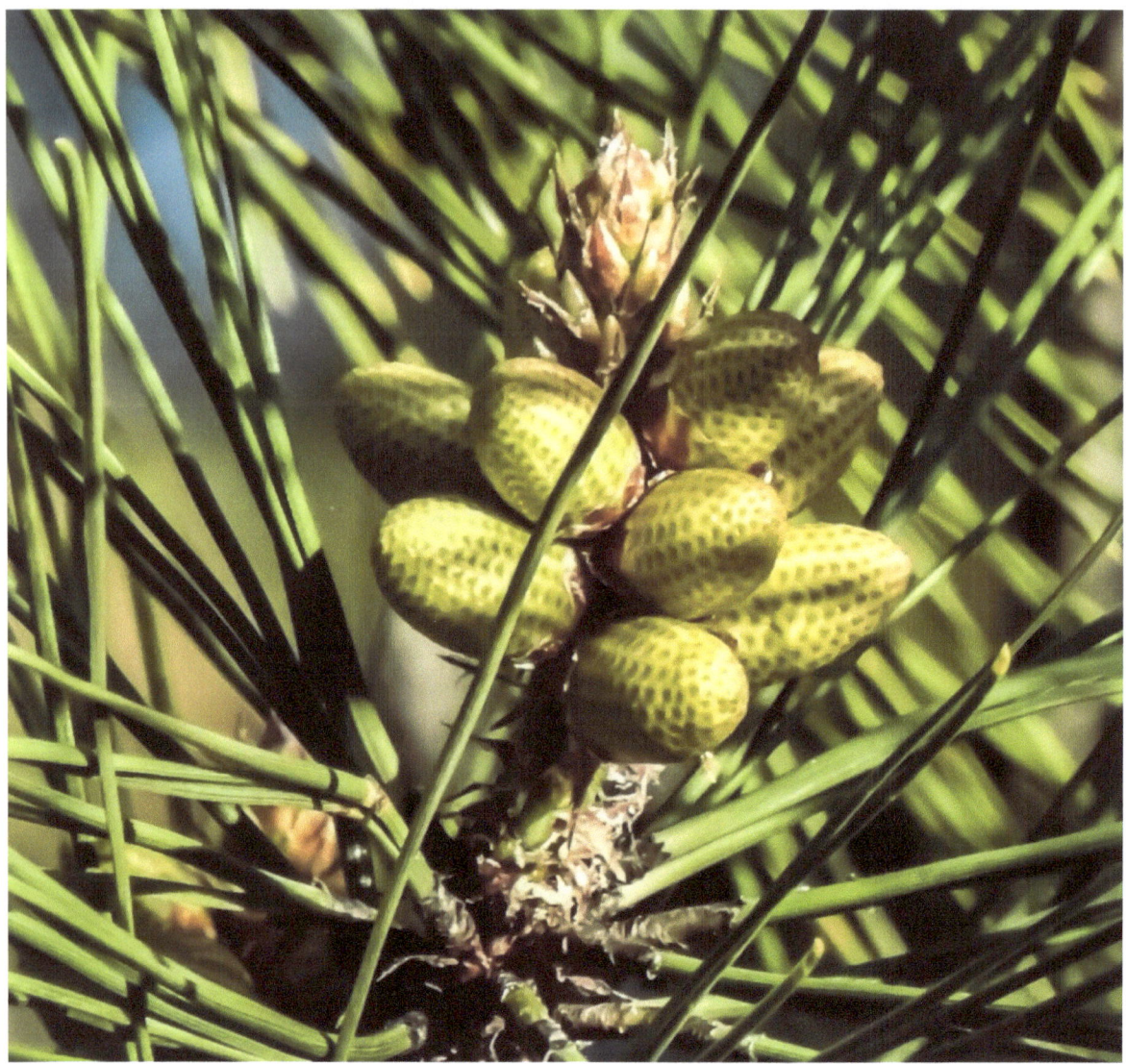

These are the buds as seen in early May that will become brown cones on Ponderosa Pines by the end of summer. Pine cones are not the seeds of the trees. They are like corn cobs in that they hold the seeds. You can also see in this picture that the variation of Ponderosa Pine that grows in the central highlands of Arizona has needles that are grouped in bundles of three.

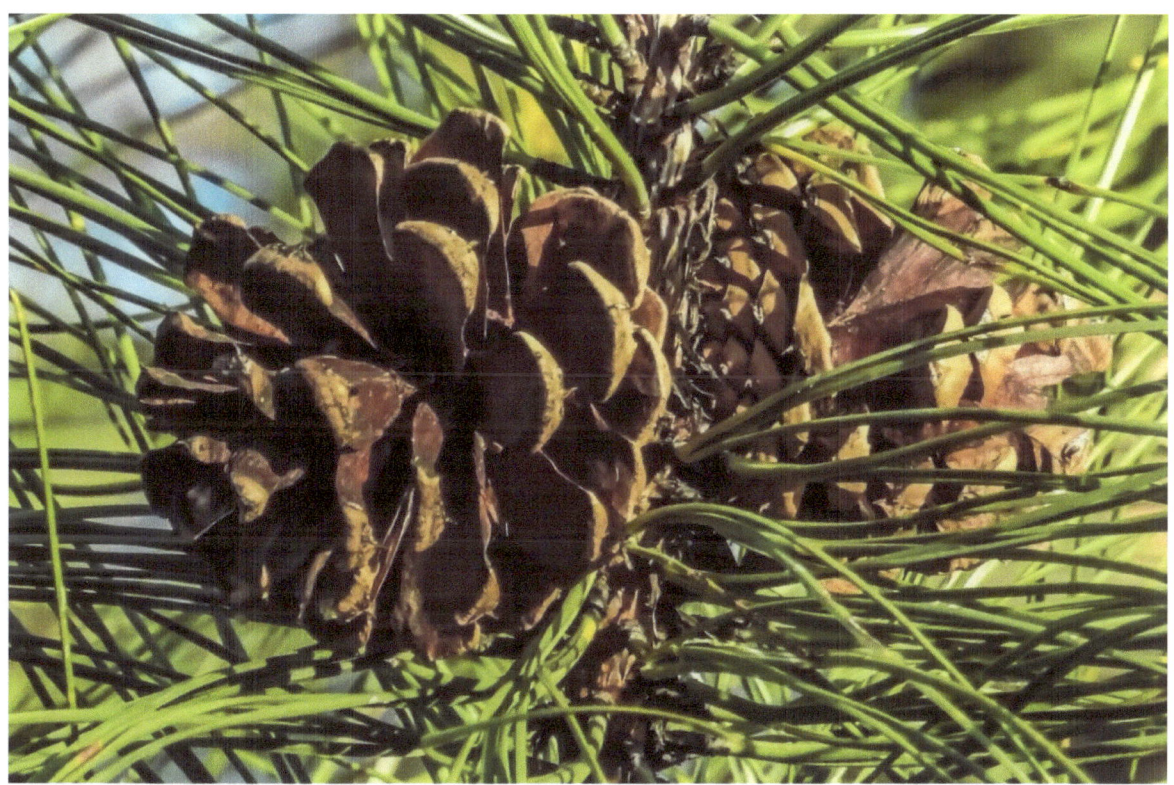

Each spring you will be able to see a few cones left on Ponderosa Pines from the previous year. These have opened and dispersed their seeds, commonly called pine nuts.

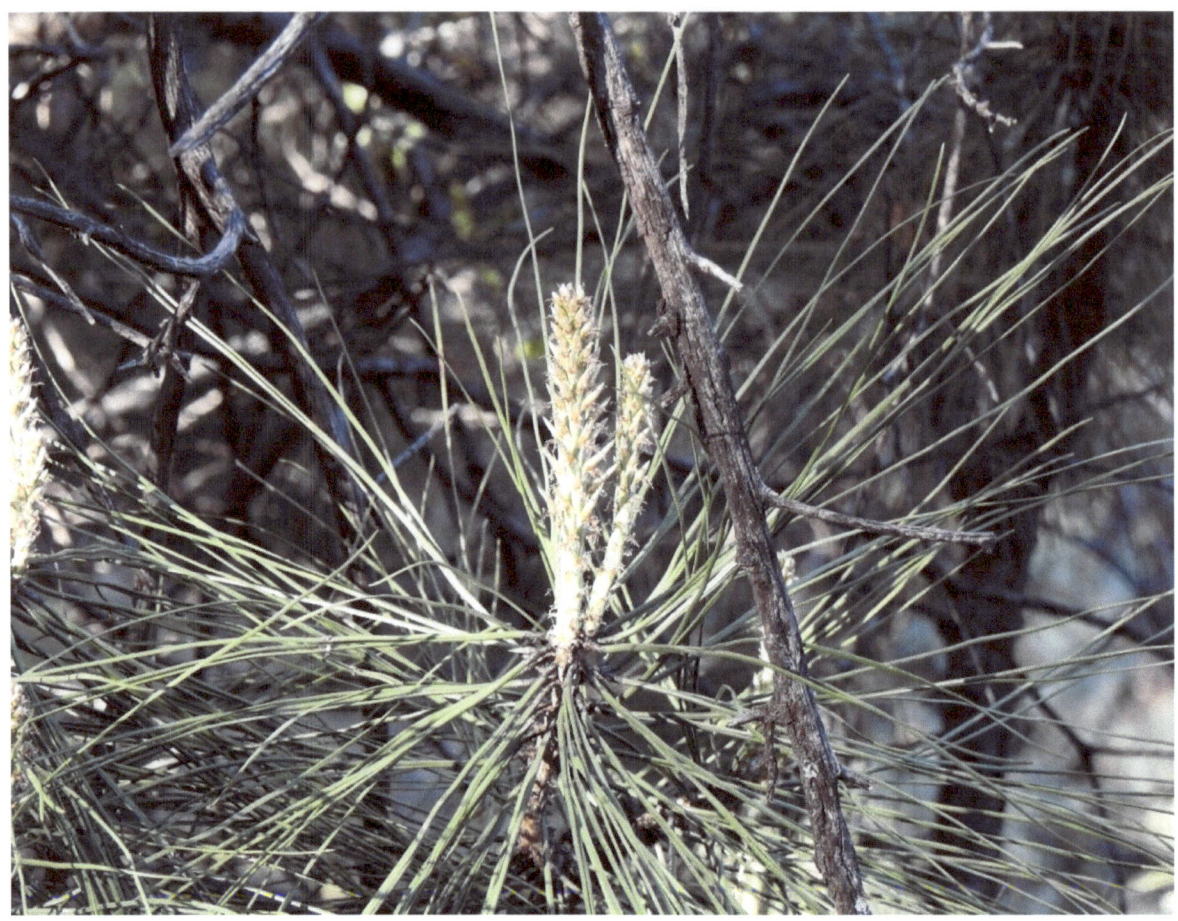

These are what is known as growth candles on Ponderosa Pines. These occur on the tips of branches. As they expand the tree will grow taller and the branches will spread over a wider area.

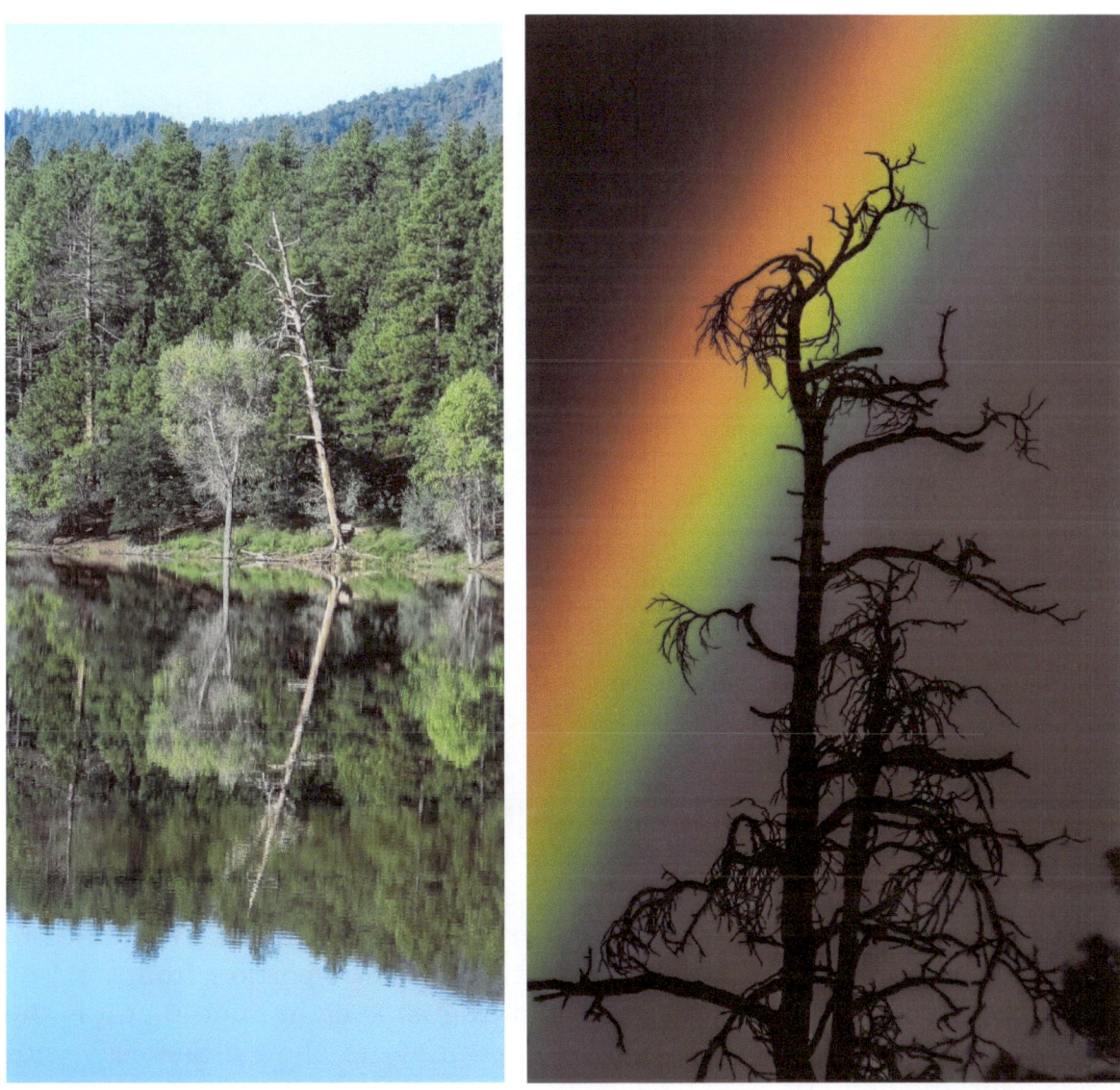

These are some examples of dead Ponderosa Pines that you might use if you are depicting a forest scene.

OAKS

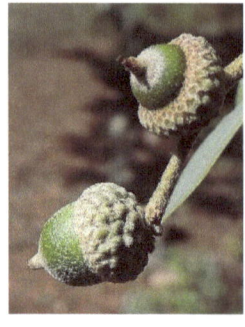 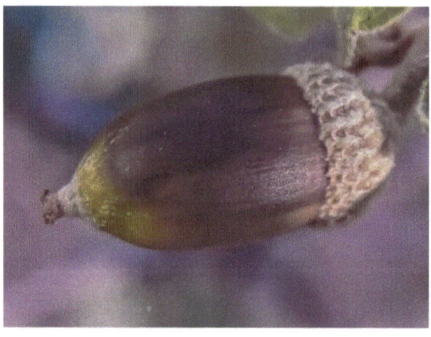 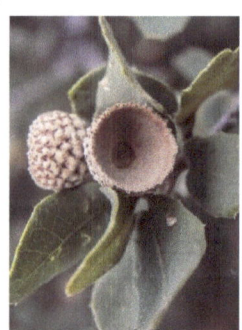

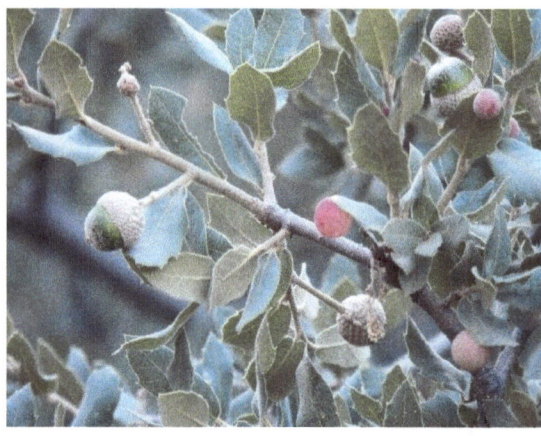

These acorns are what Acorn Woodpeckers eat in the fall and over the winter. The stage of development of those in the upper left picture is typical of mid-August. In a few weeks the acorn will turn brown indicating that it is mature. The birds can easily separate the nutritious, brown portion from its less desirable cap. If you choose to depict mid-August keep in mind that it is the monsoon season and that it could be appropriate to show a dark sky with some lightning and puddles. The lower picture shows Apple Galls on an oak with acorns. Galls are formed when insects deposit eggs in the trees and then sting the tree to cause it to produce substances that provide nutrition for the larval insects. Acorn Woodpeckers will drill into the galls to eat the larvae but they prefer to harvest the acorns.

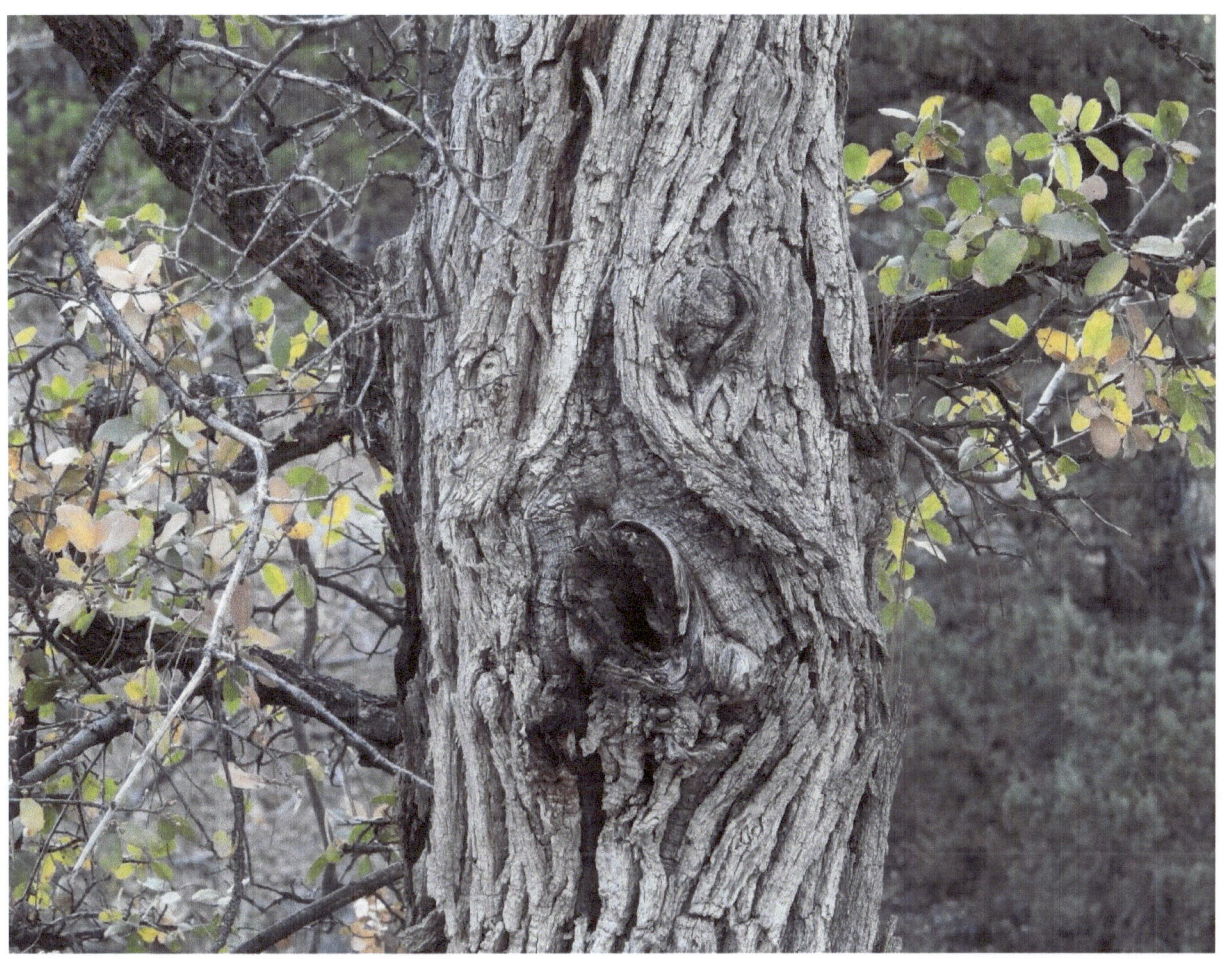

This is an Arizona White Oak. This is the source of many of the acorns the birds eat. You will often see "faces" in the bark of these trees. This tree is pictured in early May. This tree keeps its green leaves throughout the winter. They turn yellow-brown and shed as winter is ending. In early May green leaves will appear. However, acorns do not develop until later in the summer and harvested in later summer when all of the leaves are usually green.